A Voice in the Night

Copyright © 2022 by Miiko Shaffier
All rights reserved. No part of this book may be reproduced in any manner whatsoever without prior written permission from the author, except in the case of brief quotations in reviews for inclusion in a magazine, newspaper or broadcast.

BY MIIKO SHAFFIER
co-written by Chana Grosser

Illustrated by: Dmitry Gitelman (diemgi.com)
Layout & Design by: Ken Parker (visual-variables.com)

Published by:
Shefer Publishing
www.SheferPublishing.com

For permissions, comments and ordering information write:
Miiko@LearnHebrew.tv

ISBN 978-0-9978675-8-9

A VOICE IN THE NIGHT

an **EASY EEVREET STORY**

BY MIIKO SHAFFIER

SHEFER
───────────
PUBLISHING

Based on the Book of Samuel.
This story can be read like any English story book. When you get to a Hebrew word, do your best to sound it out and guess the meaning. You can check the pronunciation and meaning in the back of the book.

HAVE FUN!

To show CHahNahH how much he loved her, 'ehL-KahNahH would bring CHahNahH lots of tasty food. But CHahNahH was sad. Too sad to eat the delicious food her husband brought her.

She decided to ask G-d for a בֵּן. In her prayers she promised that this בֵּן would be a holy child, serving in the House of G-d.

שְׁמוּאֵל grew and grew and soon he wasn't a baby any more.

It was time for שְׁמוּאֵל and his אִמָּא to go on a special journey. They packed קֶמַח and יַיִן and took 3 bulls with them on their journey.

They traveled to SHeeYLohH to the House of G-d. שְׁמוּאֵל would stay in SHeeYLohH. He would grow up with 'ehLeeY the Great Cohen taking care of him in the House of G-d. One day שְׁמוּאֵל would even hear the voice of G-d Himself!

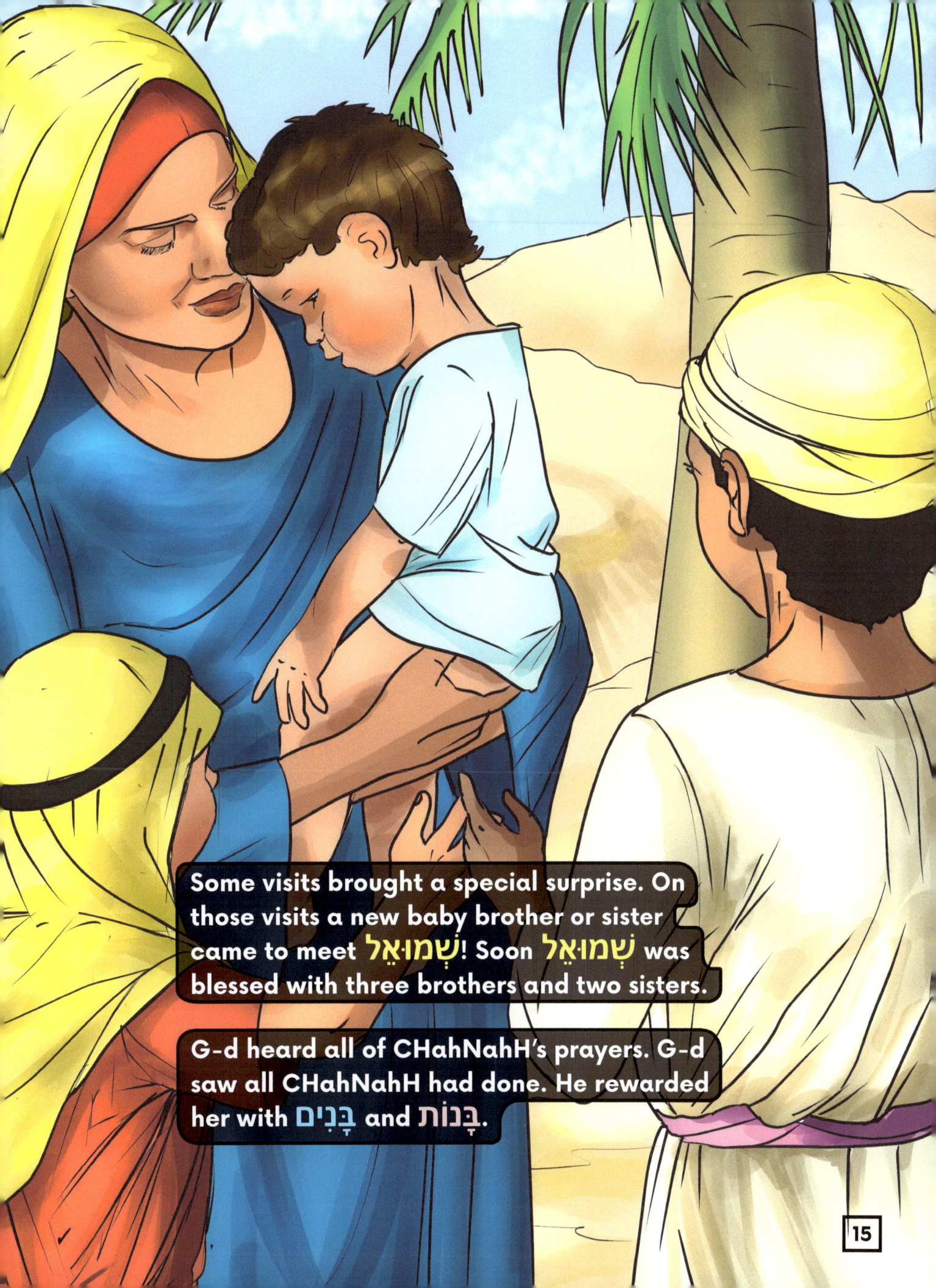

Some visits brought a special surprise. On those visits a new baby brother or sister came to meet שְׁמוּאֵל! Soon שְׁמוּאֵל was blessed with three brothers and two sisters.

G-d heard all of CHahNahH's prayers. G-d saw all CHahNahH had done. He rewarded her with בָּנִים and בָּנוֹת.

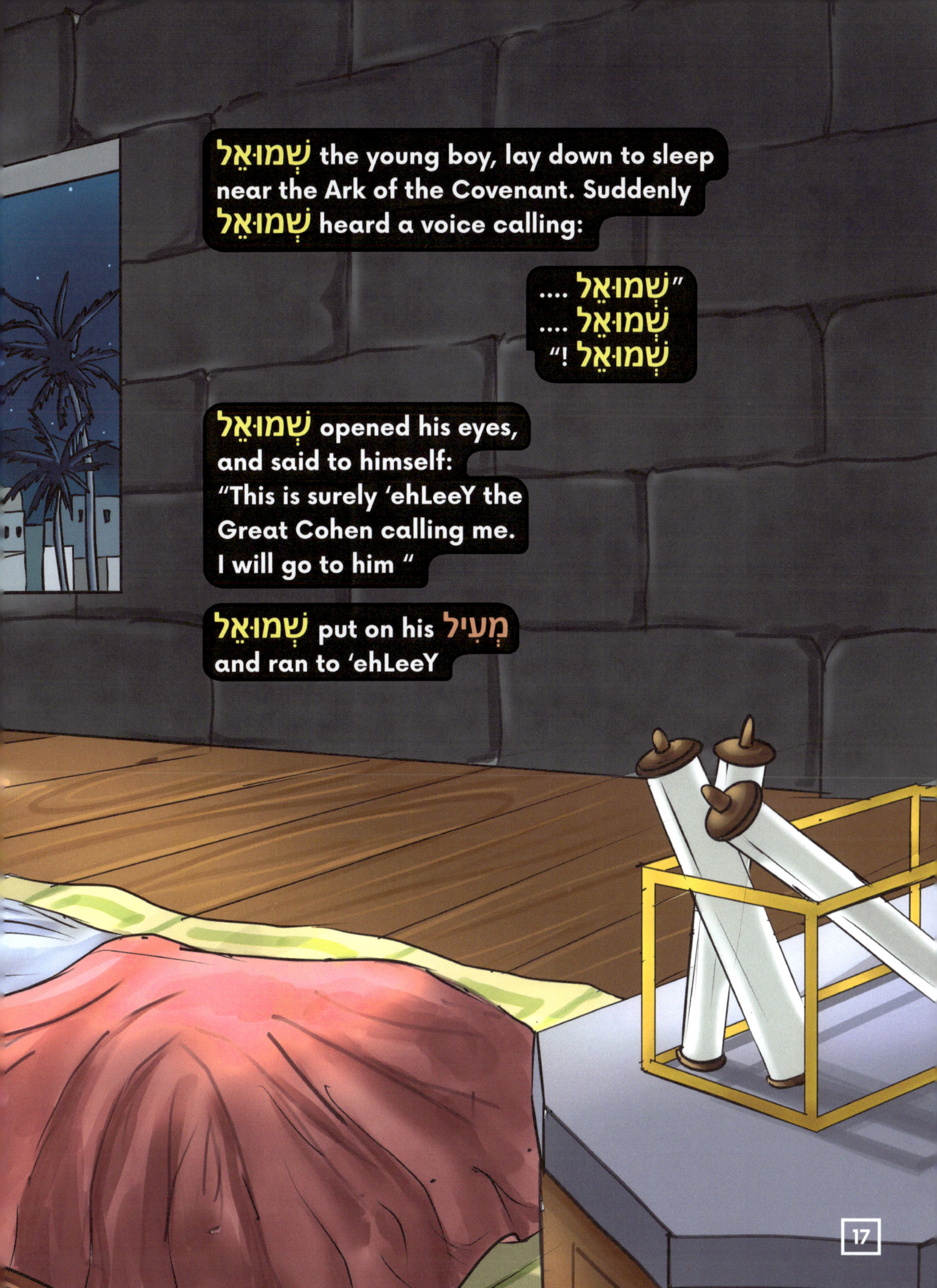

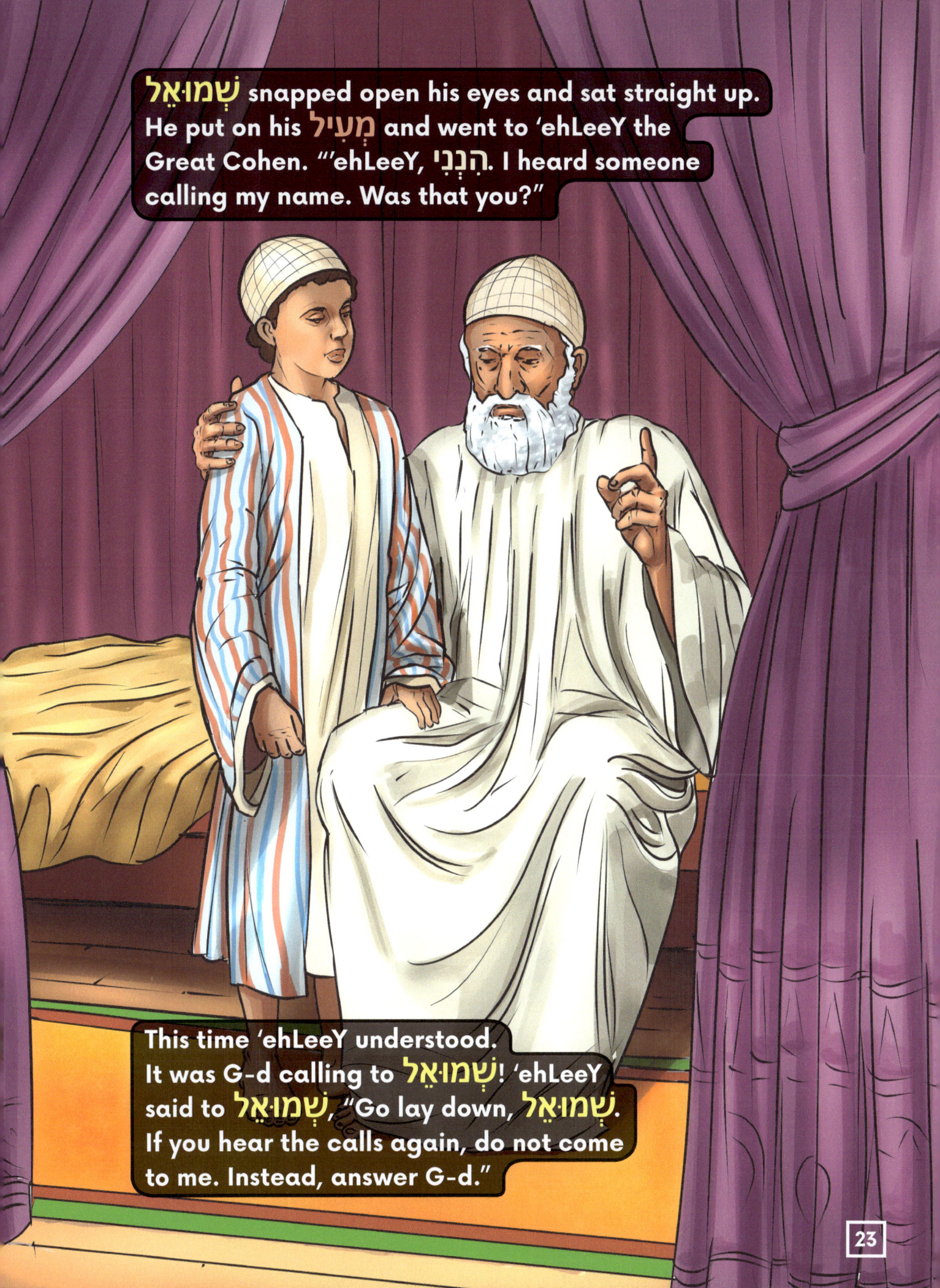

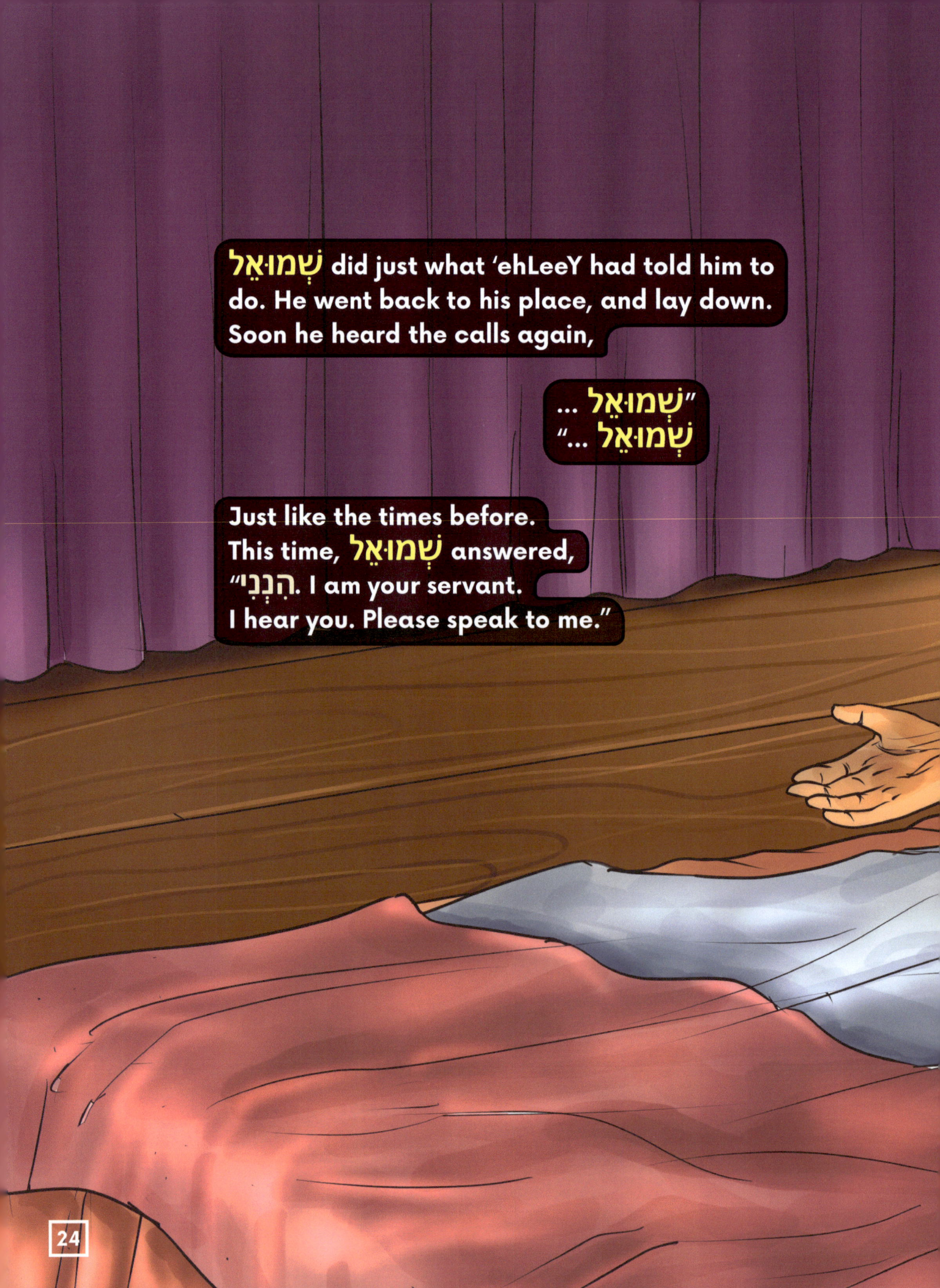

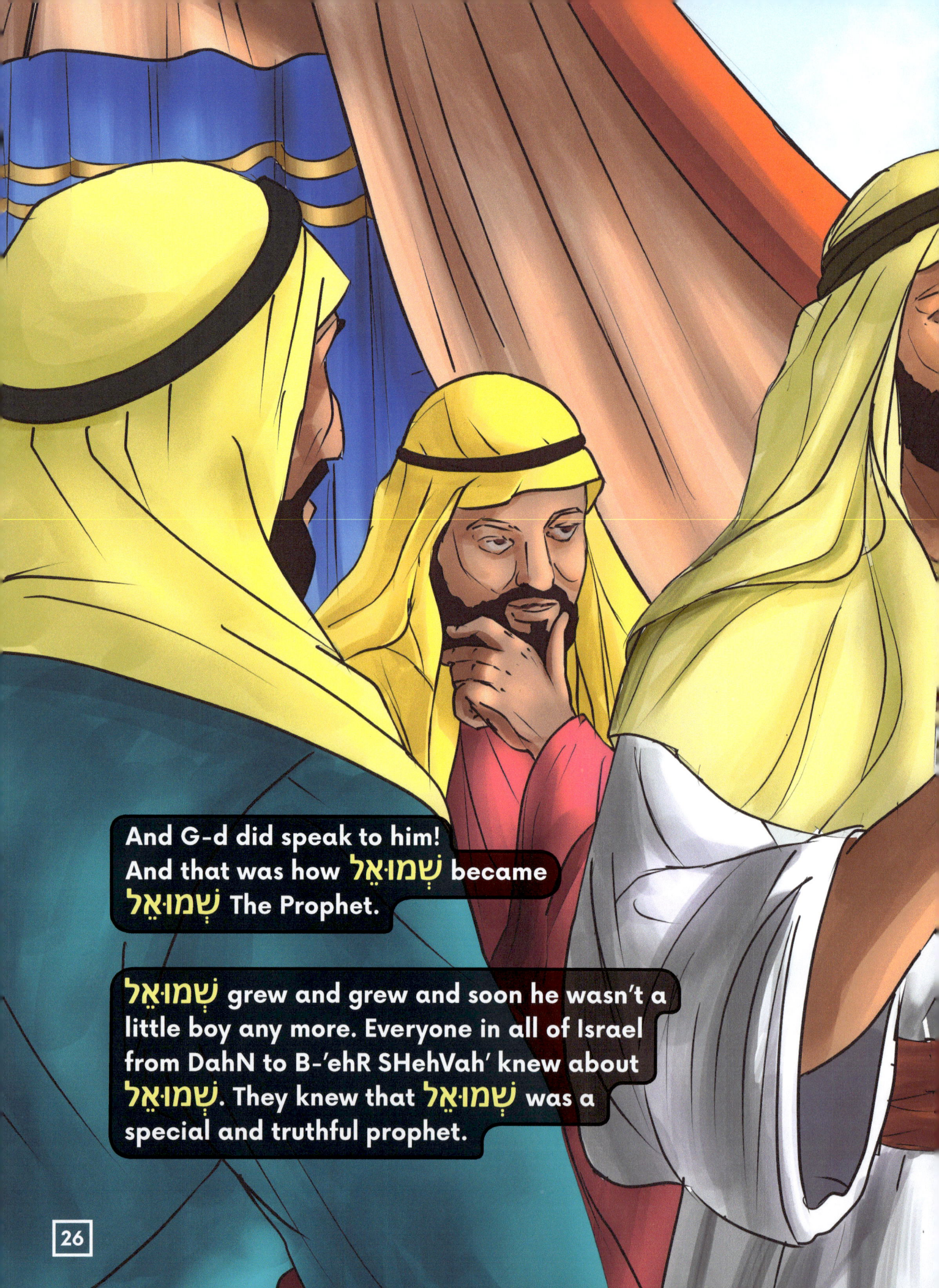

And G-d did speak to him! And that was how שְׁמוּאֵל became שְׁמוּאֵל The Prophet.

שְׁמוּאֵל grew and grew and soon he wasn't a little boy any more. Everyone in all of Israel from DahN to B-'ehR SHehVah' knew about שְׁמוּאֵל. They knew that שְׁמוּאֵל was a special and truthful prophet.

Here are the Hebrew words from this *Easy Eevreet Story*:

 'eeSHahH – **WOMAN AND ALSO WIFE** | p. 5,12

 'eeSH-Toh – **HIS WIFE** | p. 7

 LehV – **HEART** | p. 8,10

 Y-LahDeeYM – **CHILDREN** | p. 7

If it's only one child use the word:

יֶלֶד YehLehD – **CHILD (BOY)**

יַלְדָה YahL-DahH – **CHILD (GIRL)**

 BehN – **SON** | p. 8,10

 SH-Moo'ehL – **SAMUEL** | p. 10-13,15,17-24, 26,27,28

 'eeMah' – **MOTHER** | p. 12

 KehMahCH – **FLOUR** | p. 12

 YahYeeN – **WINE** | p. 12

 M-'eeYL - **COAT** p. 14,17,19,20, 22,23

 BahNeeYM - **SONS** p. 15

 BahNohT - **DAUGHTERS** p. 15

 NehR - **LAMP OR CANDLE** p. 16,20

 HeeN-NeeY - **HERE I AM** p. 18,21,23,24

 B-NeeY - **MY SON** p. 18,21

That was great reading! Let's take a closer look at some of the words we read. Notice how words change but mean **almost** the same thing.

SON - BehN

MY SON - B-NeeY

SONS - BahNeeYM
(In Israel today, teachers will call a group of boy students BahNeeYM as well)

DAUGHTER - BahT

MY DAUGHTER - BeeYTeeY

DAUGHTERS - BahNohT
(In Israel today, teachers will call a group of girl students BahNohT as well)

Hi!

My name is **Miiko.** I live in Be'er Sheva, Israel. My husband Aaron and I have nine kids: Menucha, Mendel, Dovi, Yisroel, Freida, Devora, Fitche, Geula, and Azaria.

I teach Hebrew reading with a fun little book called *Learn to Read Hebrew in 6 Weeks!*

My second book *The Hebrew Workbook* teaches readers to write in Hebrew.

A Voice in the Night is part of a series of storybooks that teach Hebrew vocabulary to kids.

I'm so pleased to be a part of your Hebrew journey. If you have any questions or want to say hi please send me an email! Miiko@LearnHebrew.tv

To the Parents

This book is designed to teach Hebrew vocabulary to people who already know how to read the Hebrew alphabet. While reading this Bible story in English you'll come across Hebrew words embedded in the text. Sound out the words and try to guess their meaning from the context. Check the key in the back of the book to see if you were right.

I've chosen to transliterate the names of the biblical characters mentioned in this story so that you'll learn the authentic Hebrew pronunciation of these biblical names.

Transliteration

A Voice in the Night uses the same system of transliteration as my first book *Learn to Read Hebrew in 6 Weeks!*

I came up with a unique transliteration system. It's designed to have the reader pronouncing the Hebrew words accurately without ever having heard a Hebrew speaker pronounce those words.

Here's a breakdown of the system:

Each consonant is represented as a capital letter and each vowel by small letters.

The silent letters 'ahLehF (א) and 'ahYeeN (ע) are represented by an apostrophe (')

The silent vowel 'Sh-Vah' (:) is represented as a hyphen (-).

An important exception to make note of:
The CH does not represent the ch sound like in *chair* or *chest*. In fact, Hebrew doesn't have the ch sound like *chair* or *chest* at all.

The CH represents the letters CHehT(ח) and CHahF(כ) and Final ChahF(ך). These letters make a sound not found in the English language. It's a chokey sound that almost sounds like a kitten purring but much harsher. Think about the name of the composer Bach. From what my Spanish speaking students tell me, it's the same sound as the guttural J in Spanish.

Let's look at the first word in the Hebrew Scripture as an example of how my system works:

בְּרֵאשִׁית

I transliterate it:
B-Reh'SHeeYT

Others may transliterate Bereshit or Bresheet but then you wouldn't know if the vowels are long or short.

If you learned to read Hebrew using my other book, you are already well familiar with this system. But in case you learned to read Hebrew elsewhere, here's a key to make sure it's clear.

LEARN TO READ AND WRITE HEBREW WITH MY FUN AND EASY SYSTEM!

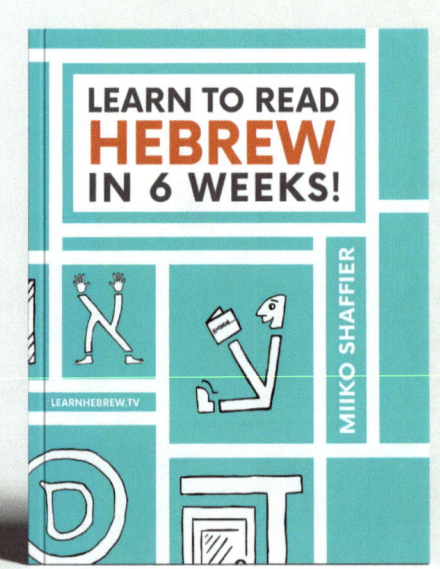 

#1 BESTSELLERS
IN HEBREW LANGUAGE INSTRUCTION

- FUN MEMORY TRICKS
- 12 SIMPLE LESSONS
- PACED TO FINISH IN 6 WEEKS
- LEARN TO READ THE HEBREW BIBLE
- GREAT FOR ADULTS OR CHILDREN ALIKE
- CHARMING ILLUSTRATIONS TO MAKE LEARNING HEBREW A PLEASURE

MORE DETAILS AT LEARNHEBREW.TV

AVAILABLE AT AMAZON

www.ingramcontent.com/pod-product-compliance
Lightning Source LLC
Chambersburg PA
CBHW041436010526
44118CB00002B/87